Late Elementary Piano Solo

Pirate's Tarantella

Catherine Rollin

Signature Series

Pirate's Tarantella

Catherine Rollin

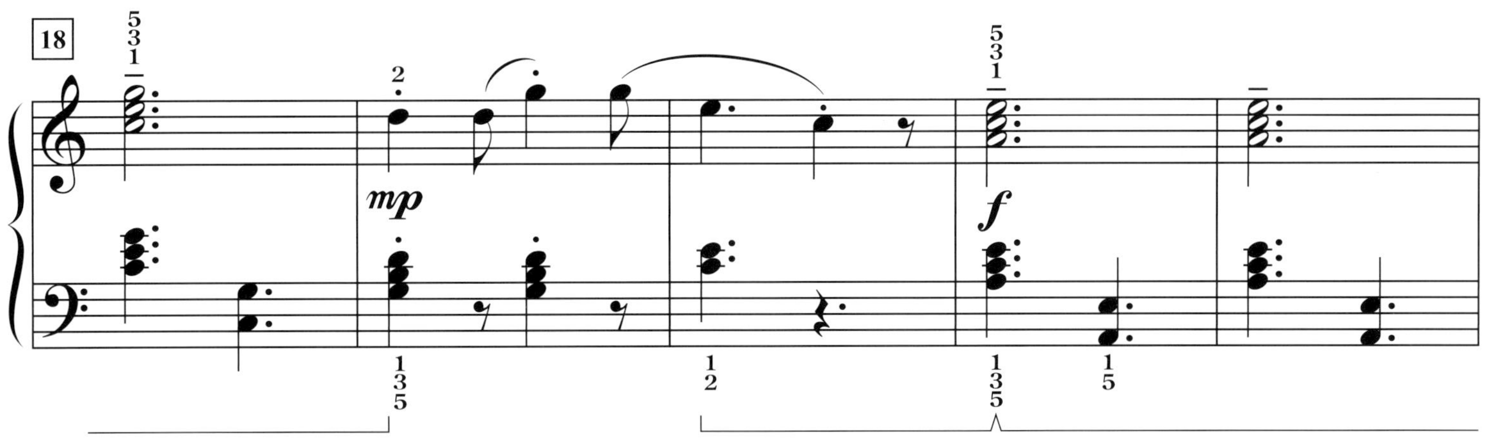
18
mp
f

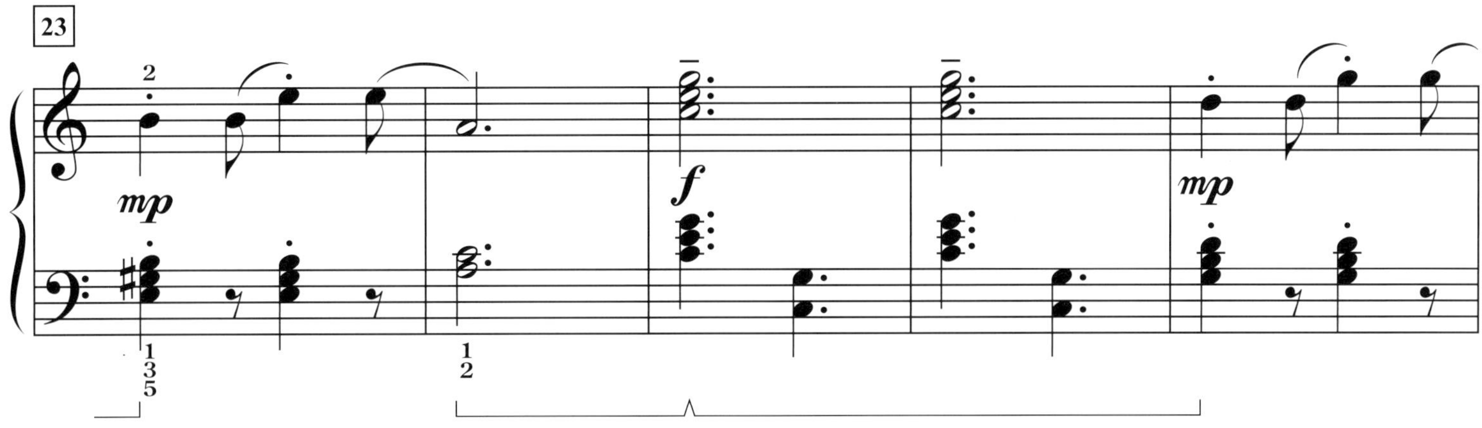
23
mp
f
mp

D.S. al Coda
28
p
cresc.
rit.
f
mp

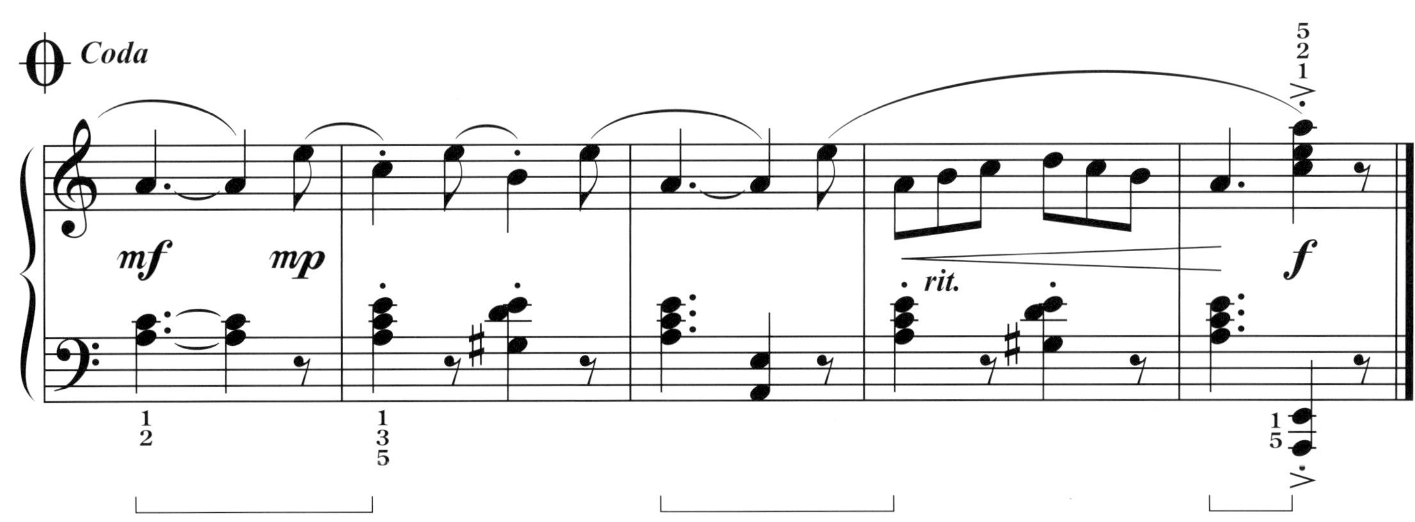
Coda
mf
mp
rit.
f

Alfred's Premier Piano Course

Dennis Alexander • Gayle Kowalchyk • E. L. Lancaster • Victoria McArthur • Martha Mier

Lesson Book

Book 1A	22356
Book 1A & CD	20652
Book 1B	22358
Book 1B & CD	22352
Book 2A	23264
Book 2A & CD	22173
Book 2B	25721
Book 2B & CD	25719
Book 3	27779
Book 3 & CD	30222
Book 4	29036
Book 4 & CD	30202
Book 5	30897
Book 5 & CD	32022
Book 6	33919
Book 6 & CD	34643

Theory Book

Book 1A	22354
Book 1B	22174
Book 2A	22371
Book 2B	25725
Book 3	28040
Book 4	30011
Book 5	32649
Book 6	34668

Performance Book

Book 1A & CD	21232
Book 1B & CD	22172
Book 2A & CD	22368
Book 2B & CD	25722
Book 3 & CD	28000
Book 4 & CD	30010
Book 5 & CD	32646
Book 6 & CD	34669

Pop and Movie Hits

Book 1A	34015
Book 1B	34016
Book 2A	34415
Book 2B	34416
Book 3	36431
Book 4	36432
Book 5	37615
Book 6	37616

Technique Book

Book 1A	27627
Book 1B	27628
Book 2A	32077
Book 2B	32177
Book 3	34105
Book 4	34106
Book 5	35261

Christmas Book

Book 1A	30878
Book 1B	30879
Book 2A	30895
Book 2B	30896
Book 3	32817
Book 4	32818
Book 5	36743
Book 6	36744

Assignment Book

Levels 1A–6	28358

At-Home Book

Book 1A	22180
Book 1B	22364
Book 2A	22365
Book 2B	25726

Flash Cards

Level 1A	22355
Level 1B	22366
Level 2A	22367
Level 2B	25727

GM Disk for Lesson and Performance

Orchestrations by Brent Mills and Jason Nyberg

Level 1A	23258
Level 1B	23259
Level 2A	23260
Level 2B	23263
Level 3	30426
Level 4	30204

General MIDI accompaniments can be downloaded at alfred.com/downloads

Success Kit

Includes Lesson Book & CD, Performance Book & CD, Theory Book, At-Home Book, and Flash Cards in a Zipper Organizer.

Level 1A	23215
Level 1B	24592

Organizer with Zipper

Clear binder w/pockets	103595

Universal Edition

The Universal Edition is designed for all English-speaking countries outside of the United States, including Canada, the U. K. and Australia.

Universal Edition Lesson Book

Book 1A & CD	23860
Book 1B & CD	23863

Universal Edition Theory Book

Book 1A	23869
Book 1B	23870

Universal Edition Success Kit

Level 1A	24437

Alfred Music

42408

US $3.50

0 38081 47305 5

Alfred

alfred.com

ISBN-10: 1-4706-1086-8
ISBN-13: 978-1-4706-1086-9

9 781470 610869

50350